LJUBLJANA

Meta Kušar
LJUBLJANA

❧

Translated by
Ana Jelnikar & Stephen Watts

Introduced by Francis R. Jones

Arc
PUBLICATIONS
2010

Published by Arc Publications,
Nanholme Mill, Shaw Wood Road
Todmorden OL14 6DA, UK
www.arcpublications.co.uk

Design by Tony Ward
Printed in Great Britain by the MPG Books Group,
Bodmin & King's Lynn

978 1904614 41 8 (pbk)
978 1904614 92 0 (hbk)

ACKNOWLEDGEMENTS
This book was first published by
Cankarjeva založba, d. d., Ljubljana, 2004.

Cover picture by Metka Krašovec,
by kind permission of the artist.

This book has received financial support from the
Trubar Foundation, sited at the
Slovene Writers' Association, Ljubljana, Slovenia,
and the Ministry of Culture of the Republic of Slovenia.

Editor: Jean Boase-Beier

CONTENTS

Series Editor's Note / 9
Translator's Preface / 11
Introduction / 18

The 'Visible Poets' series was established in 2000, and set out to challenge the view that translated poetry could or should be read without regard to the process of translation it had undergone. Since then, things have moved on. Today there is more translated poetry available and more debate on its nature, its status, and its relation to its original. We know that translated poetry is neither English poetry that has mysteriously arisen from a hidden foreign source, nor is it foreign poetry that has silently rewritten itself in English. We are more aware that translation lies at the heart of all our cultural exchange; without it, we must remain artistically and intellectually insular.

One of the aims of the series was, and still is, to enrich our poetry with the very best work that has appeared elsewhere in the world. And the poetry-reading public is now more aware than it was at the start of this century that translation cannot simply be done by anyone with two languages. The translation of poetry is a creative act, and translated poetry stands or falls on the strength of the poet-translator's art. For this reason 'Visible Poets' publishes only the work of the best translators, and gives each of them space, in a Preface, to talk about the trials and pleasures of their work.

From the start, 'Visible Poets' books have been bilingual. Many readers will not speak the languages of the original poetry but they, too, are invited to compare the look and shape of the English poems with the originals. Those who can are encouraged to read both. Translation and original are presented side-by-side because translations do not displace the originals; they shed new light on them and are in turn themselves illuminated by the presence of their source poems. By drawing the readers' attention to the act of translation itself, it is the aim of these books to make the work of both the original poets and their translators more visible.

Jean Boase-Beier

9

Meta Kušar was born on 10 May 1952 in the Mestni Log district of Ljubljana, in the house of her grandmother, and moved in 1962 to a house her parents built in Trnovo, a little closer to the city centre, where she still lives. It is a house calm with atmosphere: its kitchen, its dining-room office, its library and bedrooms, its rooms filled with books, its nooks and crannies for working in, its laundry basement and hallways, its garden complete with bicycle and, until recently, her faithful, cantankerous dog.

Meta Kušar grew up in Tito's Yugoslavia and found refuge from a regime with which she had little sympathy in books (she worked for fifteen years at a publisher's), a few well-chosen friends, the craft of language, the love of music, a sense of Slovenian culture and, from her mid-20s following the death of her mother, a deep interest in Jung, Tagore and theosophy. These latter concerns took her to India on a number of occasions.

Among writers she feels a kinship with, it's worth mentioning Marina Tsvetaeva, Vesna Krmpotič and Ralph Waldo Emerson, and among Slovene writers France Prešeren, Srečko Kosovel, Oton Župančič and Tomaž Šalamun.[1] But if she has taken anything from them, it has been more a sharing of spirit and purpose rather than anything linguistic. She herself has a forceful voice very much her own. It is worth acknowledging that she has strong friendships and affinities with people at a distance from poetry: with artists and film-makers, architects and photographers, as also with many people who live quietly in her city's anonymity and ordinariness, and that these connections are as strong a source for her poetry as anything within Slovenian literary tradition.

Ljubljana is Meta Kušar's city: it is where she has lived,

---

[1] France Prešeren (1800-1849), Oton Župančič (1878-1949), Srečko Kosovel (1904-1926), Tomaž Šalamun (b. 1941), all of them major Slovenian poets.

walked, bought – and cooked – her food, thought, written and loved. Ljubljana in all its beauty, history, modernities and anachronisms is where Meta Kušar has conducted her life, and it is a place close to her heart. She knows its buildings and its air, its Plečnik[2] market and bridges, its great Library (also designed by Plečnik), its small river and its river spirits, its ceramic ovens and convoluted detail; and she knows where those who've crossed swords – or words – with her also live. She has, of course, balanced her intense knowledge of the city with experience of other places: a small house near Rijeka on the Adriatic coast; the city of Trieste where she often worked (her essays, radio features and journalistic pieces form an integral and important part of her œuvre); visits to India in the 1990s, to Italy in particular and, more recently, to Paris, St. Petersburg and Bratislava. But it is to Ljubljana that she returns and this city, the centre of a diverse Slovenia, is her constant home and muse. It is perhaps unusual for a poet to be so inspired by one place these days; the 'rootedness' of this can give the impression of a sort of conservatism. But to read the poet or her poetry in this light

---

[2] Jože Plečnik (1872-1957) was one of the great figures of a resurgent Slovenian culture. An architect, designer and visionary, he may perhaps be best compared to Charles Rennie Mackintosh, although Plečnik was active longer as an architect, and contributed a greater number and a greater variety of finished buildings across a wider geographical area than Mackintosh ever had the chance to. It is also useful to think of Plečnik in terms of Antoni Gaudí, both of them whirling from a zone of religion and 'conservatism' at the same time as being, in Mandelstam's terms, genuinely revolutionary. One can think of Meta Kušar's poetry in such terms, though with a different emphasis. The strong and vivid imprint left by Plečnik on the city of Ljubljana is one that Meta Kušar evokes and invokes – though without directly addressing him – throughout her book. She also recalls, as a very young child, seeing Plečnik walking on the streets of Trnovo, where she grew up, and in the centre of Ljubljana.

would be quite wrong. In fact Meta Kušar's language is dense and vivid, full of contemporary tensions and visions; it achieves its sureness precisely because she manages to hold such tensions and visions together in her lucid language.

Meta Kušar didn't publish her first book until she was almost forty and her poetry – though it might come more quickly to her now – was a long time in the making, a little like the *potica* or tarragon cakes she prepares in her kitchen: she knows exactly what she is doing, but what she is doing is based on years of good experience and also on the experience of others handed down to her. One of the poems of *Ljubljana* seems almost to refer to this process directly: when she writes "like my mother before me, and other women before her, / I knead dough slowly and want it to rise well" (poem 71, p. 105), we might take this as a description of how her own words work. Her poetry, in fact, lies between language and how she experiences the world. For Meta Kušar's poetry – seen by some as unworldly – is completely, and wonderfully, of this world. We are reminded of Osip Mandelstam's words that "classical language is the poetry of revolution", except that Meta Kušar might object to the violence of revolt. Her language manages, unusually, to be both forceful and subtle at the same time – a considerable achievement.[3]

Meta Kušar published *Ljubljana* in 2004, although she had been working on the texts of the poems from 1999 through to 2002. We started translating her manuscript in 2002 and a good dozen of our translations were put on-line on the Poetry

[3] Many aspects of Meta Kušar's poetry are analysed from a feminist perspective in the English language afterword by Stanislava Chrobáková Repar in the anthology *The Voice In The Body: Three Slovenian Women Poets – Erika Vouk, Meta Kušar, Maja Vidmar* (Ljubljana: Slovene Writers Association, 2005).

International website in 2005. Over the next four years we were able to work on the rest of the manuscript, sometimes together in Ljubljana and sometimes by e-mail. We always strove to sustain a close transformation from the well-developed literals provided by Ana to what we felt might work as 'finished' poems in translation. This process tended to involve a negotiation between the literal sense in both languages and the deeper meanings of the poetry, first in Slovenian and then in English. The poet's own language, the *ur*-text of her voice, whilst seemingly dense, is in fact also very sharp and transparent. We therefore strove for such precision and clarity in our translations and, of course, this involved departing from the texts before pulling back towards them again, until they seemed winnowed of unnecessary dust. We benefited from working closely with the poet, both in Ljubljana and on the Croatian island of Hvar where the three of us were able to spend two weeks together .

*

Meta's particular vocabulary – her almost intentional avoidance of political correctness, the occasional thin dividing line between rhetoric and precision or between her focus on the word and her awareness of the 'other', her absolute individuality in the use of language – was probably the most challenging task we faced as translators, not least because words carry different connotations and emotional weight across cultures and languages. When, as in the last poem, "a barbarian" and "a nobleman" are evoked without (it would appear) any subversion of what is deeply problematic in the use of such words, the reader may feel somewhat ill at ease. To translate these words exactly as they are in the original required us to realise that the outer drama in Meta's poetry is a deliberate window onto individual inner dramas and that these concepts stand for the warring psychic entities that exist within all of us. What could appear anachronistic – her use of words such as 'hero', 'palace', 'noble', 'barbaric' – is, in fact, not so, mainly because she is using such words (and 'hero' is very apt here) in a Jungian sense and also because she locates these words in her body, in her self, and in the language of the poetry of this world and not of elsewhere. She is writing a book of Ljubljana, a city (albeit a small city) that until recent times has gone through periods of upheaval and turbulence, and she therefore invokes what she loves about the city, what she sees as strong in its past while, at the same time, very consciously writing in and of its present. That is where she is: writing something between an evocative celebration and an angry lament.

In poem 13 (p. 43) the poet uses the Slovenian word 'gverilci' for which a literal translation might be "guerrilla fighters". We resisted using this term, because it suggests particular contexts and meanings for English readers. "Partisans", a word we were drawn to because of the presence of the Partisan struggle in Yugoslav history, provoked a strong reaction from the poet, since for her the word had specific political connotations with which she was very uneasy. In terms of both the liberation struggle of the '41-'45 War and the nature of the Communist regime that followed, the word "partisan" brought to the surface too much of betrayal and pain. And yet in English the word seems to be the most appropriate to the Slovenian text. What to do? To translate is, in part, to bring to the surface of another language the language and sense of the original. In the end we opted for "resistance fighters", both to honour the poet's choice but also to avoid the resonances that the word "guerrilla" introduces into English.

In the first poem of Ljubljana the poet writes 'modra vata', the literal of which is "blue cotton". Straightforward enough. However the Slovenian word 'vata' has overtones for the poet of vatic, while the word for blue '*moder*' also carries the sense of wisdom for Slovenians. Thus '*modra vata*' is not at all the rather tepid "blue cotton" that the literal English might make of it. Looking for other options, we thought of "indigo", which seemed closer to the meaning in Slovenian for the sense of intense blue and the healing and heraldic qualities the word conjures in English.

*

The Slovenian edition of *Ljubljana* has reproductions of five paintings of the city by the artist France Kralj.[4] In his beautiful winter depiction of the city from Castle Hill, painted in 1929, Krakovo is in the middle foreground to the left and Trnovo just out beyond the edges of the canvas. It speaks to us across a wide span of space and time and its detail is almost cartographic – the city and its hills with a covering of snow, an icy red raspberry sun – and its atmosphere is both vivid and visionary. Looking at it, as such qualities seep into your consciousness, you become aware of just the same measure of light and dark in the poetry of Meta Kušar also.

Ljubljana has expanded greatly since Kralj climbed Castle Hill to paint his view of the city below, and many of its empty spaces have been built on and developed. He was at the height of his powers when Meta Kušar's parents were young, and much has changed in the city's culture since. Meta Kušar's poetry faces these injections of new culture, while trying to retain the vision and language of a still cohesive world.

The present English edition of *Ljubljana* has as its front

---

[4] France Kralj (1895-1960) was a major Slovenian artist of the twentieth century.

cover a painting from 1970 by Kušar's contemporary, Metka Krašovec,[5] which depicts a side-view of the Franciscan Church on Prešeren Square, in the very centre of the city, across the river from the wide market designed by Plečnik. The sharp sunlight-reds and shadow-dark abstraction of the painting seem to hold a city's hidden face: almost literally, if you look carefully at the lines of the shadows, but also in the sense of:

> How do I go about tidying the cosmic warehouse
> so as not to mess up its body of stars?

> (poem 18, p.47)

If Kralj's painting evokes Ljubljana as Meta Kušar might want or need it to be, Krašovec's painting shows the city coming to terms with its post-modernity, the realities that Meta Kušar knows she must inhabit and struggle to describe. "Poets are good as long as they crack / like fresh asparagus" (poem 26, p. 55). This, then, is her book of Ljubljana, her spiritual lava, both celebration and lament.

Stephen Watts & Ana Jelnikar

---

[5] Metka Krašovec (b.1941) is a major contemporary Slovenian artist.

THE POETICS OF PLACE

The seventy-seven poems that form Meta Kušar's *Ljubljana* pay complex homage to her home city, the Slovenian capital, at first sight, anyway. Which does not imply that first sight is misleading: Meta Kušar's verse starts from, and relies on, an intense seeing of the world. But her poetic world is both sight and *in*sight, inner and outer together: her verse traces the interface between surface and essence. In poem 19 (p. 49), for example, cloud and day are seen as stages in a cycle of consequence:

I watch a cloud
freely shape the day.
Trapped in the dharma of it
trying for what no other had ever done.

Moreover, in Meta Kušar's poetic world, surface is not just sight. What makes her poetry special is that she explores her world not only with sight, but also with scent, hearing, taste and touch. And this weft of five senses is shot through with a sixth: the skill of sensing the numinous beneath the normal – as in this vivid image from poem 12 (p. 41), where the sensuality of touch is simultaneously felt in hands, heart and head:

Dough rising on my hands.
In my heart and in my head
the same white flocks.

The meditative, intellectual substrate present in all of Kušar's poems combines cognition ("heart") with emotion ("head"). And it also encompasses the spiritual:

Nature's still, spirit walks about.
Under the chestnut trees and through time.

(poem 8, p. 37)

18

Kušar's vision of Ljubljana begins with places, buildings, bridges that visitors to her city also see – the Krakovo neighbourhood in poem 6 (p. 35), for instance, or the baroque church of St. Jacob in poem 40 (p. 71). Her Ljubljana is intensely real, here, experienced. But the cycle is no mere visitors' guide. This is, firstly, because Kušar's is an insider's Ljubljana. In the conventional sense, it is an intimately familiar city, since it is the city she lives and works in. But in a more essential sense, the physical space of Kušar's verse is also personal space, animate with associations and images, rich with references. Hence her insider's insight means she senses the depths and interconnections under Ljubljana's skin. Kušar's Ljubljana, therefore, is also a place of mind and memory. Plus, being the poet's birthplace, it is a place of the body as well. An extension of her body, in fact. Thus the lines from poem 8 just cited lead us into an image in which the sixth sense, spirit, links the seen city with the hand that writes:

Nature's still, spirit walks about.
Under the chestnut trees and through time
Along a shoulder to the neck.
Down an arm and onto paper.

A second reason why this work does not simply describe her city's sights lies in Kušar's slightly surrealist style. Her key technique is the associative sidestep, which constantly shifts the reading out of easy narratives and picturesque descriptions:

Seasons pass through a body and black cloud –
as into a hyacinth.
Anger goes through a flower and
drops time. Verve. Verse. Everything!

(poem 18, p. 47)

Such shifts from image into image are actually far from uncommon in recent Slovenian poetry – they also typify the works of the elder grand master Tomaž Šalamun, for instance. However, as a poet, Meta Kušar is very much her own woman. As Ana Jelnikar (one of this edition's translators) and Iztok Osojnik write:

> Kušar's poetry is concerned with testing the boundaries, pushing out the limits of language and experience, opening one for the experience of the other. If meaningful change begins where familiar collides with the unfamiliar, the subconscious with the conscious, the ordinary with the magical, the particular with the general, the finite with the infinite, and – finally – home with the world, then it should not surprise us to find her voice at once strange and familiar.[1]

A third reason why Kušar's *Ljubljana* goes beyond simple description is that it has a wider reach than a guidebook with the same title – as wide as the world, in fact. Her Ljubljana is like Borges' *aleph* – the infinitesimal, singular point in a Buenos Aires cellar where "all the places of the world, seen from every angle, coexist".[2] In poem 2 (p. 31), for instance, Kušar's Ljubljana contains whales, icebergs, and even the Aegean – though fitting it in is a bit of a squeeze: "Where can / we put it?" In poem 29 (p. 59), Ljubljana also holds Padua and Venice's Café Florian, plus, in poem 42 (p. 73), the mosaics of Ravenna:

> The four rivers of paradise have folded up.
> The sky over the house is caved in.
> On its bright rim Zeus
> is bending a thunder-bolt. Christ
> is just staring ahead.
> He wants me to take the chalice from Theodora's hands.

[1] "Poet – Meta Kušar", 2004, posted on Thezaurus / Slovenian literature – Slovensko leposlovje, www.thezaurus.com/forums/viewtopic.php?t=561, accessed December 2009.
[2] Jorge Luis Borges, *Collected Fictions* (tr. Andrew Hurley), Penguin, 1998, p. 281.

These places are not randomly chosen, of course. Kušar turns the lens of her *aleph* towards them in order to illuminate routes of cultural affinity and influence leading back to Ljubljana. "The Aegean" hints at Slovenia's embracing of the classical Greek heritage, as shown by the myth that Ljubljana was founded by Jason's Argonauts (hence the reference to the "gold fleece" in poem 7, p. 35, say). And in highlighting the cities of Italy's north-east coast, she is hinting at Slovenia's links with a wider post-Roman and Renaissance heritage that spans the upper Adriatic.

One aspect of Slovenia's heritage which Kušar does not highlight, at least not explicitly, is its seventy-odd years in Yugoslavia. The Slovenians were one of Yugoslavia's founder nations in 1918. They were also the first to leave: Slovenia declared independence in 1991, a decade before the original *Ljubljana* poems were written. What strikes me, however, as a translator of poetry from various Yugoslav regions and their successor states, is that Kušar's *Ljubljana* reflects a particularly vibrant tradition in late Yugoslav literature. This is the use of the local as a portal into the universal. Here, poets and novelists explore their own cultural geography and heritage not for their own sake, but as pathways into deeper human or existential concerns – roots as routes, so to speak. Vasko Popa's poetic retellings of Serbian myth, for example, expose the atavistic within the everyday. Or Mak Dizdar's poetic quest into the heresies of medieval Bosnia reveals the unending dialectic between faith and questioning, between persecution and hope for justice. Similarly, the locale of Meta Kušar's Ljubljana leads into a wider meditation on the links between where we are and who we are, between place, mind and body, between present experience and cultural heritage.

The Task of the Translators

Most translators, whether they work with business letters or poems, set themselves a similar aim: to make a text in a new, 'receptor' language that has the same meanings and functions as the original, 'source' text. With poems, this ideal is almost always impossible. This is because a poem, as much as a piece of marquetry, is carved from and closely follows the grain of its source material – be it the grain of grammar and words or be it the grain of shaved wood. When languages change, the grain of language changes too. A Slovenian word, say, and its English dictionary equivalent will rarely have the same sonority, rarely span the same range of associations and uses – and rarely be able to perform the same grammatical tricks. Thus subjects, indirect objects and direct objects (as in 'The banker awarded himself a bonus') are shown in English by word order and in Slovenian by noun and adjective endings, which means that Slovenian word order can be much freer than in English. And what is special about the language of poetry is that it uses all these resources of sound, meaning and grammar, and more besides. Hence Robert Frost's wry definition of poetry as that which is lost in translation – the sound, the nuance, the grain.

And yet, poetry translation happens. Translating poetry, in other words, is the art of making the impossible possible. In good translation, as this book bears witness, the poetry is not lost, but transformed. Instead of copying, translators make a new poem that resembles its source in some essential way, but which follows the grain of the new language, using the new language's resources of sense and nuance, sound and syntax.

Like other arts, poetry translation has two aspects: technical skill and intuitive decision, both of which demand high expertise. Technical skill is required not only to read and interpret a Slovenian source poem, say, whilst being alert to the potential nuances, references and associations of each phrase, but also to produce a convincing counterpart poem in English – and to integrate all this in a constant to-and-fro between reading and writing, checking back with the source and redrafting the merging target poem. Underlying all this is a web of intuitive decisions, what interpretation to give each Slovenian line, say – and what to depict in the English poem, and how. For there are no rules decreeing what of the source poem's semantics and poetics must be reproduced as closely as possible, and what can be abandoned or freely reshaped.

Ana Jelnikar and Stephen Watts, as eminent and experienced translators of poetry, have mastered both the skills and the decision-making. But their strength also comes from cooperation. The technical skills just listed are so wide-ranging that they are rarely found in a single person: poetry translators need both to be expert poetry readers in the source language and expert poetry writers in the receptor language. Slovenian native reader Jelnikar, who is both a translator and a literature specialist, and English native writer Watts, who is both a translator and a successful poet, make the ideal two-person team for this complex task.

As a snapshot of their team expertise, let's compare Kušar's poem 19 (pp. 48-9) and its translation:

Opazujem oblak,
ki svobodno oblikuje dan.
V posledice ujet
poskuša, kar še ni noben pred njim.
Deževje zapelje natančno tja,
kjer je že vse mokro.
Utrujena, izjokana in prazna pišem.

I watch a cloud
freely shape the day.
Trapped in the dharma of it
trying for what no other had ever done.
Rains drive exactly to where
it is all already wet.
Tired, teared-out and empty I write.

Following the grain of Slovenian, Kušar has built a strong assonance into the first two lines: the vowel and *consonant* chains in "O*p*azujem o*blak*/ki svobodno o*blik*uje dan" ('I notice cloud which freely forms day'). Throughout this collection, the translators closely preserve the original images, but fine-tune them so that the poetics follow the grain of English. Here they use vowel rhyme on "shape" and "day" – which is a more powerful technique in English because English has many more vowel sounds (and hence fewer accidental vowel rhymes) than Slovenian. This is backed up by the strongly iambic rhythm of both lines: "I ` watch a ` cloud / ` freely ` shape the ` day" – the most common base rhythm of English poetry. Moreover, they compensate for losing a little assonance here by gaining a little later: contrast the Slovenian "mo*k*ro. / Utrujena, izjo*k*ana in *p*razna *p*išem" ("Wet. Tired, finished-weeping and empty I write") with the sonically somewhat richer "we*t*. / *T*ire*d*, *t*eare*d*-ou*t* and emp*t*y I wri*t*e".

Sometimes the translating team take a more resolutely creative decision to reshape the original image. The lines "V posledice ujet / poskuša, kar še ni noben pred njim", mean "Captured into consequences / it tries what yet none [had tried / done] before it". Here Jelnikar and Watts, probably with the poet's approval or even prompting, render "consequences" as "dharma". This activates a resonance that is only latent in the original, but which arguably adds to the force of the poem in English.

Poetry translators, however, do not just translate poems. As the title of this series reminds us, they are almost always driven by the motive of making poets visible to new readers in another language – what Walter Benjamin called giving poetry an "afterlife".[3]

[3] "The task of the translator" ("Die Aufgabe des Übersetzers", 1923, tr. Harry Zohn), in Lawrence Venuti, ed. *The Translation Studies Reader*, Routledge, 2000.

We must be grateful to Jelnikar and Watts for making Kušar's poetry visible to readers of English. But their expertise in enabling this deserves to be made visible too. I hope that this short essay has helped to highlight the value both of the source poems, and of the translators' work in creating an English afterlife for these poems.

Francis R. Jones

LJUBLJANA

1.

Sramota in nesreča
kako drevo propada.
Mila moja rajska ptica!
Devet parov rok me odriva in drži.
Preteklost me razdira in zgradi.
Moja nevidnost je varna.
In praznik,
ki zdrsne v prvi žarek.
V celo hišo in v očeh zastane.
Se pogled podeduje?
S peresom rajske ptice.
V pesmi ni nič drugače.
Liste obnavlja.
Trnovo in palače.
Reka in večer v vrbju.
O, šumeče zvezde. Oplazite skalpele,
da bo iz konic švistnila modra vata,
ki ozdravi mrtve.
Da bodo otroci imeli prednike.
Ljubezen, prikaži se!

1.

Shame and misfortune
to see this tree decay.
My sweet bird of paradise!
Nine pairs of hands holding me up.
The past unpicks and rebuilds me.
My invisibility is safe.
And my holy day,
slipping into the first ray of sunlight.
Into the whole house, resting in my eyes.
Do we inherit it, this way of seeing?
With the plume of the bird of paradise.
It is no different in a poem.
Leaves are renewed.
Trnovo and the palaces.
The river and the evenings in the willows.
Rustling stars brush against the scalpels
so that their blades gush with indigo
to heal the dead.
So children have ancestors.
Love, be here!

2.

Kam dam Egejsko morje?
Kam kite?
Pa ledene gore? Izvire? Kam dam klavir?
Zvoki so silna narava,
kjer počivamo.
Spremstvo je zasedlo dvor
z raztreseno prtljago, ki se valja dvajset let. Še več.
Z mladostjo uničijo letino,
mesto tepejo v obraz
in kralja preženejo v smrtne igre.
Kdaj mu bo neznana sila prinesla pravo delo,
da bo spet živ?

3.

Pod vrbe si šel prisluškovat.
Sam Bog se je valil
z meglicami, ki se prijemljejo obrežja.
Reka brez vala.
Večer je dišal po topli rozinovi potici.
Bil si srečen.
Že dolgo nisi bil.

2.

The Aegean. Where can
we put it? Whales? Icebergs?
Wellsprings? The piano?
Their sounds are glorious nature
where we can rest.
Attendants have occupied the court;
for twenty years their luggage has lain scattered about.
Their folly ruined the crop,
hit the town in its face
and drove the king to deadly games.
When will an unknown force call him to work
and he be alive again?

3.

You went to eavesdrop under the willow trees.
God himself rolled with
the mist which clung to the shore.
A river with no waves.
The evening smelt of warm raisin cake.
You were happy.
As you had not been in a long time.

4.

Se ti zdi,
da mimo zakonov neba in mimo tega sveta,
še kar naprej hočem svoje?
Prosim, še mi grej zapestje.
Še pišem knjigo.
Še mešam maslo. Kavna krema se hladi.
Majhen kovček zlagam za New York.

5.

Če se sklonim pred instinkti množic,
hostija nič več ne poči.
Lepota zdrsne iz mesa.
Duh resničnosti diši razločno.
Ta pok razpoči vse navadno.
Desetletja na ustnicah lovijo sanje,
ki so zamudile običajni čas samo zato,
da so lahko prišle.

4.

Do you think
that beyond the laws of the sky and of this world,
I'd still want to have things my own way?
Please, work my wrist. Keep it warm.
I am still writing the book.
I am still folding butter. Whisked cream is cooled.
I am packing a small bag for New York.

5.

If I yield to the crowd's instincts,
the Host won't crack.
Beauty will slip out of flesh.
The spirit of reality will have a distinct smell.
This will break what is ordinary.
Decades on my lips are trying to catch dreams
which had missed their time
until finally their time came.

6.

Nočem ponavljati tistih besed!
Neka nežnost tukaj živi,
ki jo komaj dopuščajo.
Posebnosti se najprej dedujejo.
Opravki čakajo na težkih stolih.
V Krakovem skozi sonce sneg kaplja.

7.

Shiran misli na kašmir in grško morje.
Sitnari, zavit v grobe, tople šale,
ki pikajo.
V levi roki se mu vnema zlato runo.
Ga bo vrgel v reko?
Z antike skoči malodušje.
Na nunskem vrtu obleži
pod češnjami.
Ga bodo zacelile?
V tem mestu vidim dve svetlobi.
Ena se tukaj na robu vžge.

6.

I don't want to say those words again!
There is a gentleness resides here,
which almost no one gives thought to.
Idiosyncracies are the first to be inherited.
Chores remain undone on heavy chairs.
And in Krakovo snow drips in the sun.

7.

Half-starved he thinks of cashmere
and the Greek sea. He is grumpy, wrapped
in coarse, warm scarves which sting.
The gold fleece in his left hand catches fire.
Will he throw it to the river?
Out of antiquity dejection leaps.
In the convent garden he collapses beneath
the cherry trees.
Will he be healed by them?
I see two kinds of light in this town.
One is blazing up here on the edge.

8.

Narava stoji, duh pa se sprehaja.
Pod kostanji in skozi čas.
Po rami, do vratu.
Po roki na papir.
Ne znajdem se.
Dolga leta se je akustika
mojega vrta kvarila.
Prostori so odlični, čeprav zastavljeni.
Moji dolgovi so branili izvire.
Poplačala sem jih z dejstvi,
ki jih zmagovalci niso mogli
malikovati.

9.

Nisem vsak dan dualistična.
Ko eter zgosti zrak,
se knjige podrejo.
Kdo vam je rekel brati in pisati?
Nič ni brati in pisati!
Vohate vrtnice, ki dišijo skozi zid.
Kdo mi bo pomagal načrtovati prehode?
Kdo vam bo razložil renesanso cveta?
Kdo je zanetil jasne in vedre obraze?
Ti znaš zanetiti ogenj?
Že osemdeset let se otožnost ni igrala
v tihih, okroglih utah.

8.

Nature's still, spirit walks about.
Under the chestnut trees and through time.
Along a shoulder to the neck.
Down an arm and onto paper.
I am losing my bearings.
For years now the acoustics
of my garden have been falling apart.
The premises are perfect, even if in hock.
My debts have defended these roots.
I repayed them with facts
the winners were unable
to make idols of.

9.

Not every day, this dualism in me.
As ether thickens the air,
books crash down.
Who told you to read and write?
To read and write is nothing!
Can you smell the waft of roses through the wall?
Who will help me design pathways through?
Who will explain to you the renaissance of a flower?
Who has roused such clear and bright faces?
Do you know how to raise a fire?
For eighty years now sadness has not played in
the quiet, green sheds of the garden.

10.

S kakšno silo je skočil v kamniti vrt.
Prevrnil atlas. Razsul plevel.
Nosila so ga besna božanstva.
Vedel je,
vedel je za galaksije,
za galaksije, ki so kurile dediščino.
Gredice so ga držale in ogenj
in ogenj ga je hranil.
Glina je omilila udarce,
udarce zgodovine,
zgodovine, ki je pošiljala srečo,
zadrževala povodenj,
povodenj, ki bi zalila dolge grede visokih rož.
Če stopijo rože pod slap, so zlomljene.
Koliko človek zdrži!
Nebeškost vdira kar naprej
in tisti mesec, zloščen
in strt.

10.

With what force he leapt into the stone garden.
Knocked over the atlas. Strewed weeds everywhere.
Driven by furious gods.
He knew,
he knew about the galaxies,
about the galaxies bonfiring all heritage
His flower beds gave him sustenance and the fire
and the fire nourished him.
Clay softened the blows,
the blows of history,
history which gave out happiness,
kept floods at bay,
floods which would engulf beds of tall flowers.
If flowers walk under a waterfall, they break.
How much can one bear!
Heavenliness invades time and again.
and that month, polished
and broken.

11.

Literati so naredili dosti fars
in ženske so jim pomagale.
Modri diamant
pa se preoblači nepričakovano.
Dvorjenja v navideznih prostorih
so šla v zrak.
Kača staro kožo pušča v tihi noči.
Na čipkastih otroških kapicah se je nabrala rosa.
Odbojnost je
ljubezen.

12.

Poslušam sapo, ki buta v les.
Zvesti labod pošilja hlebe kruha.
In sladke pozdrave na luni pripisane.
Rastline s poganjki so nevarne
in čutnost boli,
če ni točna.
Testo na rokah vzhaja.
V mojem srcu in v glavi so enake
bele jate.
Plahe.

11.

Men of letters have cooked up countless farces
and women helped them out.
But a blue diamond
will put on a different set of clothes.
Courtships in fictitious places
go up in smoke.
At dead of night a snake leaves its old skin behind.
On lace-rimmed children's caps dew has collected.
Refusal is
love.

12.

I listen to breath hitting against wood.
A loyal swan sends loaves of bread.
And sweet greetings attached to the moon.
Plants with offshoots are dangerous
and sensuality hurts
if it's not precise.
Dough rising on my hands.
In my heart and in my head
the same white flocks.
Startled.

13.

Se spomniš pesmi: 1983
Če bo treba sklicati gverilo,
ali bodo tudi nam,
kakor našim očetom in dedkom
jemali iz okrvavljenih prsnih žepov
Prešernove Poezije?
Sežgi jo.

14.

Iz pozabljene misli zraste slovesno dejanje.
Sprosti srce, ki je pritisnjeno med verz in strast.
Dokaz bo tu čez tisoč let.
Zato rojstva v neskončnost vztrajajo.
Ne vidim ga, ki bi vstal
prepasan
in kakor pripravljen za pot.
Na jutranjem soncu je zimska lepota bežna
in svečana.
Na pečatnik!

13.

Do you remember the poem: 1983
If once more we need resistance fighters,
will they still find Prešeren's Poems
in our bloodied pockets, as they did in
our fathers' and grandfathers' breasts?
Burn it.

14.

From forgotten thoughts, gala words emerge.
They untense a heart crushed in verse and passion.
Proof will be here, in a thousand years.
Births will last through to infinity.
I don't see anyone who would rise
girded
as though about to set out.
In the morning sun, winter beauty is short
but festive.
Here, a signet ring!

15.

Težko je spraviti vase zvonike in grbe,
ognjišča, oraklje, zlato, oblikovano esenco domačih gora.
Ne tisto,
ki v visokih votlinah nevidna sije!
Nadležni tolažniki me grabijo
in se oklenem debla.
Je hrast?
Prosim, ne prevrni mi pravice!
Tempelj je ne bo obnovil!
Samo kdor more zadržati besede
in smer,
jo bo.

16.

Bele lilije stresejo med pušpan star spomin.
Bela kava se kadi.
Pehtran vsujem v štruklje.
Zanosne besede med kamne,
liste na dno neba.

15.

It is difficult to take in belfries and insignia,
hearths, oracles, gold, the formed ore of home mountains.
Not that of tall caves,
glowing invisibly!
Bothersome consolers snatch at me.
I make it to a tree and cling on.
Is it an oak trunk?
Please, do not trample my rights!
A temple will not restore them to life!
Only someone holding to words
and direction
can.

16.

White lillies scatter memories over yew.
Café au lait steams.
I sprinkle tarragon over the dough.
Ecstatic words amid the stones,
leaves on the bottom of the sky.

17.

Judje hočejo znamenj, Grki modrost,
moja atma izbere Mestni log.
Ko je na robu barja že rasel vrt za brata,
so z nizozemskih miz izginila poglavja,
da sem jih spet lahko zagledala v orehovi omari,
med tesno zloženimi kozarci
malin, marelic, hrušk.
Ob beli posteljici,
kjer so ležale jopice,
vesel žoržet, mehak muslin in svež pike.
V krošnjah hrastov, nad modrimi planjavami žafranov.
Opazujem sliko,
ki se iz moje duše že tisočletja ne premakne.

18.

Letni časi grejo v telo in črni oblaki –
kakor v hijacinto.
Jeza gre v cvet in
osuje čas. Veselje. Verz. Vse!
Kako v astralu mimoza diši?
Kako daleč potrpljenje sveti?
Kako naj pospravljam kozmično skladišče
naroda, da ne razmečem njegovih zvezd?
Kje so ljudje, ki se niso dotaknili prekletstva?
Njihova nesmrtnost
je res originalna.

17.

Greeks like wisdom, Jews portents,
my spirit's breath chooses the city woods.
On the marsh edge a garden for my brother,
episodes of my life from the Dutch tables.
To see them again in this walnut cupboard
amid closely stacked jars,
raspberry, apricot, pears.
Next to the white cot
little cardigans strewn about,
happy georgettes, soft muslins and fresh piqués.
Through high oak branches, above the blue of saffron.
I'm watching a painted image which has
not stirred from my soul in thousands of years.

18.

Seasons pass through a body and black cloud –
as into a hyacinth.
Anger goes through a flower and
drops time. Verve. Verse. Everything!
How does a mimosa smell in the ether?
How far does patience throw off light?
How do I go about tidying the cosmic warehouse
so as not to mess up its body of stars?
Where are the people who haven't touched damnation?
Their immortality
truly is original.

19.

Opazujem oblak,
ki svobodno oblikuje dan.
V posledice ujet
poskuša, kar še ni noben pred njim.
Deževje zapelje natančno tja,
kjer je že vse mokro.
Utrujena, izjokana in prazna pišem.
Duh je hud.
Nimam stavka,
če se ga v hipu ne domislim.
Kaj naj z osamljenostjo svojih bratov?
Zanemarjenostjo njihovih trdnjav?
Nič več ne slikajo žerjavov.
Cvetoči slak jih briga kot tisti paradiž.

20.

Mislec je, svetovljan.
Jasnovidec ga spozna med mestnimi palačami.
Okusi ga izdajo,
zato si upa
preizkušati milino v zaraščenih vrtovih,
preizkušati bridkost in mračni smoter.
Pozna pristanišče, demona, ki nas je kalil v isti peči,
kjer so skovali večne, umrljive in junake.
Samo pogleda na bele planine
in srebrn vrč se napolni s krizmo.

19.

I watch a cloud
freely shape the day.
Trapped in the dharma of it
trying for what no other had ever done.
Rains drive exactly to where
it is all already wet.
Tired, teared-out and empty I write.
Spirit's angry.
I don't have the words
if I don't think of them on the spot.
What should I do with the loneliness of my brothers?
With the slovenliness of their strongholds?
They no longer paint storks.
They care as much about flowering bindweed as this paradise.

20.

He is a thinker, a man of the world.
A clairvoyant recognizes him amid town houses.
His likes give him away,
that is why he dares test
what is most delicate in overgrown gardens,
what is bitter, its dark purpose.
He knows the heart-place, the demon purging us through the same fire,
where they hammered out gods, mortals, heroes.
He has only to look out onto the white pastures
and the silver jug fills with chrism.

21.

Kako grozno je izgubljati dediščino
resničnega človeka.
Hlapci na konjih, knezi pa peš.
Bi rad živel enostavno?
Poslušaj jo.
Znova in znova je arija lepa.

22.

Toplo je. Taščica molči.
Na hrastu posluša ščinkavce.
S kljunčkom drobi usodo v zgodovino.
Ne razločim natančno vseh vrstic.
Vseh slik, ki bodo še prišle.
V hramih je hlad.
Šele, ko na belih šalih spoštovanja
zadišijo vijolični cvetovi, odleti.

21.

How terrible to lose the share
of being human.
Hirelings on horseback, princes on foot.
Do you think you can live that simply?
Listen. Over and again
the aria is beautiful.

22.

It is warm today. The robin's not singing.
On the oak it listens to a chaffinch.
Its beak is crumbling the fate of history.
I cannot make out all of the script.
Nor the images yet to come.
In the house of god it is cold.
Only when there's a trace of violet
on the white scarves of respect
          does the robin fly.

23.

Na gladkih kamnih stoji galeb.
Spomin se vstopi prav tako
preden zleti.
April ga presune, ko se razcveteni
dan zmrači.

24.

V drevoredu kostanji cvetijo,
človek pa s krepostjo vrača hudo.
Ne težkaš kamnov.
Nič ne grabiš.
Nič ne obrezuješ.
Gledaš in trpiš.
Srce junaško govori in po gubah steče
usmiljenje.
Besede so na sredini zraščene, misli pa
vdirajo, kakor hočejo.
Po suhih, sivih viticah glicinije se zgodovina
vije na dolg balkon.
Zjutraj se vsuje čez.

23.

On smooth rock a seagull stands.
Memory settles in the same way
before it flies off.
April pierces it to the quick, as the blossomed
day goes to dusk.

24.

In the avenue of trees, walnuts are in blossom,
and man with his inner strength reacts to hardships.
You are not weighing stones.
You are not grabbing at anything.
You are not trimming anything back.
You watch and you suffer.
The heroic heart speaks and your wrinkles
glisten with compassion.
Words are stitched together, but thoughts
break in as they will.
Along dry, grey tendrils of wisteria
history climbs out onto a long balcony.
In the morning it tumbles over.

25.

Zvezde se nagnetejo v solze in popacajo jopo.
Koliko zvezd!
Na sanjskem vrtu pod Gradom se utrinjajo,
zjutraj jih naberemo polne pladnje.
Spreminjajo se v borovnice, objeme, buhteljne,
v poetični prah, ki pade po trpljenju,
po načrtih in klavirju.
Samo neke pesmi dihajo.

En dan je bolj resničen od drugega.

26.

V spomin se zapletam,
v čute, in tavam.
Zakoni so,
vendar jih ne poznam.
Opazujem skozi veje,
veter in meglo.
Skozi petunije in verze.
Na stari skodelici
se nekaj nabere
in zdrsne vame.
Pesnik je dober, dokler poka,
kakor špargelj.

25.

Stars huddle into tears which smear a cardigan.
How many stars!
They plummet into the dream-garden under the castle,
and in the mornings we gather them in bucket-fulls.
They turn to blueberries, kisses, hot-cross buns,
into the poetic dust which falls on suffering,
on future plans and on pianos.
Not that many poems breathe.

Some days are more here than others.

26.

I tangle myself in memory,
in my senses, and I drift.
Laws exist,
but I do not know them.
I am watching the wind and the fog
through the branches.
Through petunias and lines of poetry.
On an old cup
something gathers,
and slips inside me.
Poets are good as long as they crack
like fresh asparagus.

Pod odrezane veje shranim dneve
in večere.
Sijaj jih dvigne,
kadar hočem.
Nič več se ne zaganjam z vso močjo.
Naj kraljica spremenljivih želja
vzdržuje svoj dvor. Naj zrači palačo.
Obsoja dogodke.
Težko
razumem,
a
vem,
da
usoda
je.

18. 11. 1948

27.

Under cut branches I lay up my days,
my evenings.
Glowing light raises them
when I want it to.
No longer do I hurl myself with all my strength.
Let the queen of fickle wishes
maintain her court. Let her air her palace.
Let her condemn everything.
It is hard
for me to understand,
but
I know
that
destiny
exists.

18. 11. 1948

28.

Logika ni prva, čeprav je prijetna.
Nekje med pogumom in čaščenjem
mi učenost pljuskne
čez rob.
Čeprav masivne palače nabirajo trajnost,
jih mraz razpoka do krvi.
Biti z življenjem eno, čeprav ne živiš!
Ogrnjen v pled, ki ne bo spustil zime v kri,
zagrabiti pečat
in ga podati!

29.

Padova razpada.
In Caffe Florian.
Pošlješ šoferja,
ki na molu San Carlo opreza, ker ne ve,
kaj pomenijo tvoje besede:
Mogoče bo v belem, mogoče v črnem
in smeje se.
Snubci čakajo,
da bo ena izmed palic čudežno ozelenela.

28.

Logic doesn't come first, though it eases things.
Somewhere between courage and worship
my learning breaks
over the brim.
Although massive palaces pile up permanence for themselves,
cold will crack them till they bleed.
To be one with life, even if you do not live!
Wrapped in a plaid which won't let winter enter your blood,
to grab a signet
and pass it on!

29.

Padua is falling apart.
And Café Florian.
And you order a chauffeur
who is looking about at the pier of San Carlo,
because he doesn't know what your words mean:
She may be in white, she may be in black,
but for sure she'll be smiling.
Wooers are waiting
for one of the branches miraculously to flower.

30.

Puščavski pesek navidezno poslabša
biografijo.
Možje bežijo v Babilon, da bi našli stavke,
ki jih razume sto milijonov pokončanih živali.
Poznam to majhnost,
ki pade v pesem zato,
ker nihče ne gleda prstov.
Nihče v obraz!
Ker ne vedo, zakaj so stavki tu.

31.

Kaj naj s hrepenenjem, če ne rastem?
Bela potonika je poklic.
Bela je močna kakor rdeča.
Čisto sama na vitraju posuši kesanje,
da barve zažarijo.
Naklonjena svetlobi, jih v trenutku oživi.
Pogum se zablešči na porcelanu in monogramih.
Pade na topli mahagonij.
Ko objame jezik in usodo,
se vroči pesek na dvorišču zakadi.

30.

Desert sand seems to sully
your biography.
Men rush to Babylon to find words
understood by a hundred million slaughtered animals.
I know the smallness
that a poem falls into when
no one bothers to see your fingers.
Or look you in the face!
Because they don't know why words exist.

31.

What's the use of yearning, if it doesn't incite growth?
A white peony is a vocation.
White as vivid as red.
Simply there in the glass it dries repentance away
and the colours flare up.
Open to its light, they blaze forth in an instant.
Courage blushes the porcelain and monograms,
and falls on warm mahogany.
When it embraces language and fate,
gravel in the driveway is churned and sent flying.

32.

Kdor pozablja piše.
Na precejenem mleku se nabira pričakovanje.
Vidim, kako smetana razvršča narode,
čeprav sanjajo.
Samo nad predana mesta zaplava debel duh.
Prerojeni ga nosijo,
vendar ne v doline,
kamor luč nikoli ne posije.
Kjer rdeče lilije ne cvetijo.
Nepredvidljivi stvori so krivi,
da ptice ne vedo,
kaj peti.

33.

Globino jezik zazna.
Pa temo vrtnice.
Njen mir, ki ne goji zaslug.

Če enost samo zavoham,
odženem nesrečo.

32.

Who forgets, writes.
On strained whey expectations form.
I can see how cream gives order to nations
even as they dream.
Only over devoted towns does thick spirit coil.
Those reborn carry it,
but not into valleys
where light never shines.
Where red lilies won't blossom.
It is the fault of unpredictable creatures
that birds don't know
what to sing.

33.

Language senses depth.
And the dark of a rose.
And a calm that doesn't prize honours.

If I get only a whiff of unity,
I drive misfortune away.

34.

Ko se zdani, pesmi utihnejo.
Mesto postane majhno.
Na smaragde skočijo ambicije,
ki se ne morejo dotakniti majske rose,
ne Jakoba Schella,
njegovega bogastva in darežljivosti,
ne kozmogonije umorjenih palač.
Ničesar zelenega.
Rudnik pod plemiškim vrtom
vali zlato, ki ga ne kujejo.
Raztresena pamet podira
bele potke in vedre besede.
Zagrenjenost zastrupi grobove
in neskončne količine zraka.
Plamenček na oltarčku skoraj ugasne.

35.

Vztrajna zmota ima svoj plan.
Ljubezen, ki jo slišim,
ni druga.
Prav ista je.
Ena in edina.
Prvi zakon stvarjenja.

34.

When day dawns, songs go quiet.
Ljubljana becomes small.
Emeralds spark on ambition
which cannot touch May dew,
nor Jakob Schell,
his wealth and generosity,
nor the cosmogony of murdered palaces.
Nor anything green.
A mine under the nobleman's garden
kneads gold which stays unhammered.
Scattered wit wrecks
white paths and serene words.
Bitterness poisons the graves
and huge blocks of air.
A little flame on a little altar almost
            flickers out.

35.

A persistent glitch has its reason.
Love which I hear
is not a different love.
It is the same love.
One and only.
First law of creation.

36.

Mesto ima ladje in morje,
ki se preoblači v reko,
da zaceli naše rane.
Roparji hočejo, da ljudje kljuvajo črnilo,
ne pesniki, ki delajo mavrico.
Njim jemljejo kroglice nabitega jantarja,
da ne bi molili in prerokovali.
Vidijo, kako gre ponoči prostor dol
in pada. Pada kar naprej.
Kdo ve, zakaj je zjutraj ogrlica še bolj žareča?
Papir še bolj bel?

37.

Nabiti, kunštni kalini se guncajo,
skrbi pa jejo najlepše cvete.
Drugačne pesmi zrastejo,
če vsak dan gledam vrt.
Zelo drugačne.
Glasove merim z odmevom, vladavine tudi.
Zato ne štejem ovac in ne iščem pastirja.
Stolnici sonce raztaplja zvonik.
Nebo doni. Hodniki v vročem zraku
trepetajo. Prsti so se mi zlepili.
Resnica pa poje, nagnjena na vzhod, poje.

36.

Ljubljana has ships, and a sea
which is dressed as a river,
so it can heal our wounds.
Thieves want people to pick at ink,
not poets who make a rainbow.
Robbed of pellets of charged amber,
they can neither pray nor prophesy.
But see how at night space diminishes,
slides and falls. And keeps falling.
Who knows why in the morning necklaces are
so lucid? Paper more white?

37.

Cheeky, punchy bullfinches bounce on branches
and worries eat up the most beautiful blossom.
Different poems grow
if I watch the garden every day.
Very different.
I measure voices against their echo, governments too.
I don't count sheep, I'm not looking for a shepherd.
The sun is melting the cathedral's steeple.
The sky booms. Corridors shudder
in the heat of the day. My fingers glue together.
And truth sings, tilted towards the east, it sings.

38.

Pod gradom se v bezgovem zraku
ziblje dan.
Srce se umika v spopad.
Čutne besede zavarujejo oboke in baldahine,
ta čas ko skregani obrazi skačejo
naravnost v domovino.
Kradljivci lepote ne vedo,
da Božja črta ni nikoli ravna.

39.

Na starem marmorju počiva lastovka.
Zemlja se trese.
Čaka, da se bo spremenil v kruh.
Kje je sfinga, ki razume, vidi, ve?
Moram zdržati
izgubljeno opojnost!
Zapuščeno skladišče cimeta diši še dvesto let.
Vročo glavo naslonim na slonovo glavo.
Kje je Indra? Nebeški Kralj? Jezus, si v labirintu?
Tisti, ki jejo sonce, so ga prehodili.

38.

Under the castle in a sway of elder
the day gently rocks.
Heart withdrawn into conflict.
Sensual words protect arches and baldachins,
now that brawling faces lash
out at the homeland.
Such thieves of beauty don't know
that a God's line is never straight.

39.

A swallow rests on old slabs.
The earth trembles.
She waits for it to marble into bread.
Where is the sphinx who knows, sees, is?
I have to endure
this loss of euphoria!
An abandoned storehouse of cinnamon
remains sweet for two hundred years.
I lean my heated head against the elephant's.
Where is Indra? The Celestial King? Jesus, are you in the labyrinth?
Who eats the sun has walked through it.

40.

Pride dan, ki je določen
za črnega kralja in belo kraljico.
Velika vrata se na stežaj odpro.
Po jezeru plavata in v popoldanskem soncu
stražita unum mundum,
ki se med kamni pretaka v knjige in zenice,
v začetke misli,
ki stro netukajšnji večer.
Beneška kompozicija ne podre idiličnega življenja,
ki zraste v čutih.
Bojim se zate, ugrabljena Evropa.

Francescu Robbi v cerkvi sv. Jakoba, 1723-1733

41.

Lahko potegnem črto?
Bom zdržala, ko se bodo posledice ujele z dolžnostjo,
ali bom padla na trnje?
O, dihati nežen, sladek mir.
Vedeti, da ni nič nikoli izgubljeno.

40.

This day comes foretold
for the black king and white queen.
Let the heavy doors roll wide open:
they will be swimming in the pool of the afternoon sun,
guardians of the one world
that seeps through rock into books and eyes,
into the beginnings of thoughts
crushing the absent evening.
Venetian proportions do not shatter idyllic life
which merges from the senses.
I am afraid for you, kidnapped Europa.

To Francesco Robba, in the church of St. Jacob, 1723-1733

41.

Can I draw the line?
Will I hold out when the consequences coincide with duties,
or will I fall on thorns?
O, to breathe sweet, gentle balm.
And know nothing is ever lost.

42.

Štiri reke paradiža so se zvile.
Nad hišo je udrto nebo.
Na njegovem svetlem robu Zevs
napenja strelo. Kristus
samo strmo gleda.
Hoče, da vzamem kelih iz Teodorinih rok.
Ne dovoli, da bi se mi na notesih nabiral led.
Poznam bitja, ki valijo hlad
in grobo, surovo snov norosti.
Mračne pohabe polepšamo s pogledom v oči.
Zastokajo kakor siti dojenčki na prsih.
A si kdo upa vzeti plašč, ki ga ponuja Elija?
Besede so, besede,
ki gorijo.

43.

Rod za rodom stoji v vrsti
za kovinski sijaj,
ki ga kovači ne cenijo.
Ker ločijo med zlatom in zlatom.
Ker njihov beli sin s tresočo roko
dvigne hrano za tujce, da bi postali bratje.
Oče jim v oranžnem plašču meče jasminove cvetove.
Psi, ki ležijo v malabarskem pesku,
debeli od vročine, odložijo garje
in lakoto in pritečejo k igri. Vsem se nam med zobmi
nabere sladek, dišeč pepel.

42.

The four rivers of paradise have folded up.
The sky over the house is caved in.
On its bright rim Zeus
is bending a thunder-bolt. Christ
is just staring ahead.
He wants me to take the chalice from Theodora's hands.
He won't let frost gather on my notebooks.
I know those who roll the cold,
raw, uncouth material of madness.
Dark malformations are improved by being looked in the eye.
They whimper like babes sated at the breast.
Will anyone dare take the coat proffered by Elijah?
These are words, words.
And they burn.

43.

Generation after generation stand in line
for the metal glow
that blacksmiths don't cherish enough.
Because they distinguish between gold and gold.
Because their white son with a shaky hand
raises bread for strangers, so they might become brothers.
Father in an orange coat throws them jasmine blossoms.
Dogs lying on the Malabar sands,
bloated from the heat, put aside their mange
and famine and run off to play. Sweet, fragrant ash
gathers between our teeth.

44.

Kljunček pobira roso
in ne pušča nobenih sledi.
Ribnik nadzira pota deklic, njihov obup.
Med metanjem kamenčkov se nad krošnjami
zberejo dišave in se razlijejo na mesto.
Vonj pokaže, kje je drsela mesečina.
Pazila bom na jezik.
Na barju Feniks ne leti.
Na gostem oblaku se pripelje.

45.

Pa še kako ima pokrajina pomen.
Ni samo prostor. Vse barve so zraven.
Na okroglih zrcalcih visijo s petja.
Na vrtnicah stražijo vso noč in me branijo.
Prepelice, z mano posute, pripeljejo dvorec.
Vem, da bo led počil.
Vem, da bo počil.
Vem, da krona uresniči napovedi.
Vem. Mrzlo petje najbolj boli,
še bolj kot čas, ki ga odriva v gnezdo.

44.

A little beak is picking up dew
and leaves no trace behind.
The pond watches over the paths of young girls, their despair.
While they are skimming stones, perfumes gather
above the treetops, and spill across the town.
The scent shows where moonlight has been gliding.
I will watch my tongue.
In the marshes, the phoenix cannot rise.
It floats in on a thick cloud.

45.

Landscape has tremendous meaning!
It is not only space. All the colours are there.
On small round mirrors they dangle from the morning song.
They guard roses through the night and they protect me.
Quails, scattered with me, brought the manor house.
I know ice will crack.
I know it will.
I know this world will crown its promises.
I know. Cold singing hurts the most,
more even than time forcing us back into the nest.

Na vsej koži, na celi pameti čutim
temo. Ko sekajo akacije, se sliši levje rjovenje.
Junak zmaga, ko se mu ne mudi.
Drevesa se bodo obrasla nad njegovimi
koraki. Dejanja so čudeži.
Potrpite cvetovi!
Prišli smo z vseh strani neba,
da bi govorili zvestobi ob žerjavici.
Zgodbam mraka.
Do svita.

46.

All over my skin, through my entire mind I can feel
darkness. When they are cutting down acacias, you hear lion roars.
A hero will win when he is not in a rush.
Trees will push up where
he trod. Deeds are miracles.
Have patience, flowers!
We have come from all the corners of the sky,
to talk to loyalty by the fire's embers.
To dusk stories.
Until dawn.

Zakleti brezdomci sekajo sveta drevesa,
drobijo plemenite oboke,
so vladarji in uveljavljajo svoj red.
Stoletja so možje spraševali listje o domu,
o milih obrazih srca.
Smo vsi klicali sovražni preobrat usode?
Ukazujejo maščevanje, prezirajo ogenj hiše,
ogenj mesta, ker vedo,
da Hestii dvorijo bogovi.
Ženske požirajo zvezde.
Njihovi fantiči razbijejo brezmejno.
Jaz pa še kar gledam gor v nebo
in kurim ogenj s starimi gospodi.
Varujejo nas zublji mistikov, jeleni, sloni,
psi.
Jagnje in labod.
Lepopisje vrtnic, lilij, krošenj, ptic.
Človek sešteva vse mogoče,
a kar je izven srca, je neskončno usodno.

47.

Those sworn to homelessness are felling sacred trees,
pulverizing noble arches,
they are rulers, enforcing their dominion.
For centuries men asked leaves about their home,
the dear faces of their hearts.
Did all of us call for the hateful turn of fate?
They command revenge, despise the fire of the house,
the fire of the town, because they know
that Hestia is courted by gods.
Women are swallowing stars.
Their boys shatter what is limitless.
But I carry on looking up in the sky
and burning the fire with old gentlemen.
We are protected with the tongues of mystic fires,
stags, elephants, dogs.
Lambs and swans.
The calligraphy of roses, lilies, treetops, birds.
Man is adding up all possible things,
but what is outside the heart is crucial.

48.

Resni delavci potrebujejo usmiljenje.
Tvoji in moji.
Zvok, ki spremlja izvoljene,
je najbolj sladek.
Ne bomo častili stare hudobije,
ker ne pozna milosti.
Zlatar gleda samo zlato.

49.

Resnice so minirane z osebnostmi.
Tudi želje in poljubi.
V atomih ostanejo stoletja cela,
tudi v celicah in verzih.
Mesto jih obnavlja v poletni krošnji,
v mrzlih iglicah, trdnih obrazih!
Okus se pojavi spontano,
kadar koli, vsepovsod,
brez zunanjega vpliva.

48.

Serious workers deserve pity.
Yours and mine.
The sound which accompanies the chosen
is sweetest.
We will not worship past mischief
that has in it no notion of mercy.
A goldsmith watches only gold.

49.

Truths are blown open by charisma.
Desires and kisses too.
Whole centuries remain alive in atoms,
also in cells and words.
Ljubljana rejuvenates them in lush canopies,
with cold needles, with steadfast faces!
Taste rises spontaneously,
at any time, all over,
without external influence.

50.

Drugi svetovi niso tam zato,
da bi jih opazovali.
Če prideš tja, delaš!
Črni mojstri preverijo tvoje srce kakor beli.
Pazljivo nas razvrščajo.
Glas, ki nas kliče, pa je en sam. Tukaj in tam.
Dar lahko povsem preide,
če ga kar naprej ne varuješ.

51.

Napuh ni hudič,
samo paličica Luciferja je,
ki pokaže,
kje bo kdo stavil.
Ko razsodnost zdrsne, se luč prestavi.
V naročju spet zagledaš zrnje, ki si ga že luščil.
Lažje je najti ogenj v kremenu,
kakor pot v zvezdah.
Oče je rekel:
Roke imaš kot kmetica.
Poljubil jih je in umrl.

50.

Other worlds aren't there
for us to observe.
If you get there, you work!
Black masters check your heart
in the same way white masters do.
They line us up carefully.
There is just one voice calling. Here and there.
A gift can be passed over
if you don't watch over it all the time.

51.

Pride is no devil,
only Lucifer's wand
showing who will
bid what.
When judgements slip, light shifts.
In your lap you again see grains you have already husked.
It is easier to find fire in flint
than a path through stars.
Father said:
Your hands are a farmer's hands.
He kissed them and died.

52.

Je res ni nihče častil?
Ne osvojil srca?
Zato lahko iz minute
v minuto razkriva zvijačo!
Milino!
A ne razumeš doma?
Ne iščeš spanca?

53.

Legenda ni pripovedovala,
da bo značaj umoril središče mesta.
V Trstu tudi ropa, a povsem drugače.
Na Dunaju ga miri stara modrina.
Pesnik nima dvoumnega orožja.
Ne upirajo se mu jeklo, srebro in kositer.
Pokaže prapore in se zarastejo rane.
Nima izgovorov.
Nima obljub.
Ve, kdo je.

52.

Did really no one honour her?
Win her heart?
Because of that she can reveal
different wiles from minute to minute?
Graces!
Don't you understand home?
Aren't you sleeping there?

53.

Legend did not say
that temperament could constrict the town's heart.
In Trieste we are plundered too, but so differently.
In Vienna it's made calm by the old blue.
A poet's art is not ambivalent.
Not repelled by steel, silver, tin.
A banner and his wounds heal.
Neither excuses.
Nor promises.
He knows, he is.

54.

Pesem je usmiljenje.
Ne čistost.
Vztrajnost je.
Križ ne.
Ker je bila prej.
Dosti prej preden steber
ozeleni.

55.

Manjkajo mi mogočni komični stavki.
Ko se gledava z luno,
ko opazujem vrtnico,
si ne upajo blizu.
Bog današnjih dni ima rojstni dan.
Ima take stavke.
Ima prihodnost, ki je sedanjost.
Ima sedanjost, ki je večnost.

23. november 1999

54.

A poem is mercy.
Not purity.
Persistence.
Not a cross.
Because it has been that already.
Long before: a stalk
turning green.

55.

I lack strong comic lines.
When the moon and I are face to face,
when I watch a rose,
they don't dare come close.
The god of this day has his birthday.
He has such words.
He has a future, which is the present.
He has the present, which is eternal.

23 November 1999

56.

Oblačila se mu svileno svetijo. Nista ga zmotila
ne slava ne prezir. Pesniki ga ne bodo nikoli
dohiteli, ker so sebičneži.
V trebuhu so mesije, v srcu
brez sočutja. Izkušnja pozna izkušnjo.
Ko na belem perju pozabiš besede,
morajo zjutraj goste
in močne ležati na oltarju.

57.

So megle, ki se nikoli ne razkadijo,
vendar jih sonce posuši.
Kje stoji dom? Ga je trpljenje zmedlo?
Te bo lastna kri spoznala?
Mlade siničke sredi vprašanj cvrčijo.
A naj jih hranim a naj letim z njimi?

56.

His clothing gives off a worn glaze. Neither
fame nor contempt disturbed him. Poets will always
be left behind, because they are egoists.
In their stomachs they are messiahs, in their hearts
without compassion. Experience begets experience.
When on the white feathers you forget your words,
in the morning they will lie thick
and solid on the altar.

57.

There are fogs that never disperse,
but the sun mops them up.
Where is home? Was it perplexed by anguish?
Will your own blood recognise you?
Baby tits chirrup in the midst of questions.
Should I feed them or learn to fly?

Izmučena sem,
pa samo na hitro listam njuno življenje.
Bila sta čarovnika, še preden
sta me rodila.
Kdo še pozida ognjišče, ki se na pragu ne konča?
Kdo pride na mojo gostijo vseh barv in omik?
Še sedaj čutim glas,
ki je kuhal borovnice.
Boj zamenja konje, ker zdržijo manj kakor pogum.
Tačas, ko v pečici kolački cvrčijo,
smrt ostro zadiši. Razpre nosnice in ostane.
Mesece prereže. Dolžino vseh stvari.
Ta zmota pretenta vse organe, samo srce
gre po svoje, ker je kri vizionarska,
kadar ni zastrupljena.

58.

I am worn out,
so I only quickly flick through their life.
The two of them were magicians, even before
they gave me birth.
Who nowadays would still build a hearth that does not end
     at the threshold?
Who comes to my feast of all colours and cultures?
Even now I can still feel the voice
that stewed blueberries.
Switch horses in battle, because they endure less than courage.
While Easter buns are sizzling in the oven,
death gives off a pungent smell. It widens the nostrils and stays.
It cuts through the months. The length of all things.
This misconception deceives all bodily organs, only the heart
has it his own way, because blood is visionary,
when not poisoned.

59.

Cvetoče jablane mi pokažejo, da je pod njimi
veliko mest nagnetenih. Razpihujejo jih
do trnovskih zvonikov in še naprej
na stopnjišča, ki so v knjigi hiš natančno popisana.
Sreča naredi oči nenasitne.
Vsako noč se mesta vračajo pod drevesa. Preveč je
davnega in pradavnega, včerajšnjega,
preveč za smrt, ki je v loncu belo posuta
in zavržena. Kje so sli, da jim ukažemo,
kar je treba?
Naj pridejo, naj pečejo kruh! Sadijo jablane!
Naj pomirijo zrak!

60.

Hiše stojijo na pesku, izsušene so in požgane.
Beduina ne privabijo kovine, marmor in steklo.
Bistrost ga pokliče. Žuboreča in sveža.
Na tihem vrtu si odmotava glavo in pripoveduje
o cvetju iz davnih pokrajin.
O ženskah, ki jih rodovi niso pozabili.
Brez predsodkov kaže njihovo rast
in svoj obraz. Duša dvojčica
pride k njemu, ker ju vodnjak razvozla.
Opazujeta se v enakih razdaljah,
zato redkeje padeta in hitreje vstajata.

28. maj 1949

59.

Blossoming apple trees show me that behind them
there are many towns clotted together. Their blossom
blows as far as the belfries of Trnovo and further
to the stone steps where in the book of hours they are noted.
Happiness makes our eyes insatiable.
Each evening the towns come back beneath the trees.
There's too much of the prehistoric, of what was yesterday's,
too much for death which is whitely strewn in an urn and
discarded. Where are those couriers, that we can tell
them what needs doing?
Let them come and bake bread! Plant apple trees!
Let them appease the air!

60.

Houses stand on sand, parched and burnt.
A bedouin's not lured by metal, marble or glass.
He is summoned by freshly rippled lucidity.
In a quiet garden he uncoils his scarf,
recounting flowers from the ancient lands.
And women not forgotten by time.
Openly he is praising their spirit.
And his own face. His soul-twin
comes to him, because the well's unravelled them.
Observing each other in equal measure,
they're slow to fall, faster to rise.

28 May 1949

61.

Spovedniku se v ustih topi hostija.
Tudi pri meni ležijo vsi čuti na jeziku.
Ko mu pustim, da se zave bogastva,
je neusmiljen.
Vzdihuje.
Rada zasadim zobe v kaj sladkega, kakor Anglež.
Koliko dela, da se velika, zakajena peč zablešči.
Da se na lošču spet zasveti morje,
na oblinah nebo.

62.

Pojmi visijo po omarah.
Misli so natlačene pod posteljo,
v kleti, na podstrešju, na balkonih,
v vrtni uti.
To so kašče.
Moka. Ne ješ je z žlico kakor močnik.
Si jedel med? Si dobil amrito?
Pomembno je, kdo bere.
Opoldne se naredi noč, da pisec počije.
Nasloni se na gazelo, posluša stepe
in žabe v rečnem blatu.
Kadar sanja o plemenu, ki je šlo v pastirico,
se strese po vsem telesu.

61.

A host is melting in a confessor's mouth.
With me, too, all sensation lies on the tongue.
When I let it become conscious of the excess,
it loses all pity.
It exults. And then, like an Englishman,
I want to sink my teeth into something sweet.
What great works for a primed-up oven to blaze.
For its glaze to reflect the seas,
and its curves, the sky.

62.

Concepts hang in closets.
Thoughts are crammed under the bed,
in the cellar, the attic, on balconies,
in the garden shed.
These are our granaries.
Flour. It's not eaten with a spoon as porridge is.
Have you had honey? Did you bring *amrita*?
It is important who reads this.
Night comes at noon, so the writer may rest.
He leans against a gazelle, listens to the steppes
and to frogs in the riverine mud.
When he dreams of his tribe changed into a shepherdess,
shudders pass right through his body.

63.

Poezija nič ne umira. Orfej je tam, kjer je bil.
V meni se sestanejo prijatelji,
v mestu se objemajo stoletja.
Jezus je naredil bratstvo za vse,
toda narava ostaja aristokratska.
Učenjaki ga ozko gledajo, kmetje mu slepo sledijo.
Širna voda je mir, po kateri pride.
Z verzom v sredo križišča.
Kako čovek vsak hip živi tudi v večnosti!

64.

Hudobni veter mi poškoduje besede.
Naj se z mečem spopadam z njim?
Polomljeno življenje se celi
od znotraj navzven.
Sredi marjetic zraste velika beseda,
na kateri zavihra zastava.
Navdušenje ji piha naravnost v obraz.

63.

Poetry is not dying. Orpheus is where he's always been.
Inside me, friends gather,
in the town centuries embrace.
Jesus created brotherhood for everyone,
but nature will always be just for the few.
Scholars narrow him, peasants follow him blindly.
The wide water is calm along which he comes.
With a verse writ in at every crossing.
How in every moment you also live eternity!

64.

An evil wind has damaged my words.
Should I counter it with a sword?
A broken life heals
from the inside.
Amid daisies, a powerful word blossoms
and unfurls its flag.
Delight blowing straight into its face.

65.

Oblika in obdobje se raztapljata.
Kaj je s hišo,
ki nima dlani za svetlo solzo?
Kjer duša ne razvije svojega telesa, tudi črke
v svitku obledijo.
V krvi smo človeški, zato ne pride vanjo manj,
kar se ima zgoditi.
Ogenj je ogenj.
Poje kot požar.

66.

Baročni srci se po tihem upodobita.
Kako napisati kesanje? Slavo?
Udariti s svinčnikom? Okusiti živo vodo?
Natisniti palačo in duha?
Kako vem, da mi besede zgodbo natančno
režejo? Kadar omahnem v navado,
samo prepisujem življenje.
Tiger ni nenavaden, zajtrkovati z njim je razbliniti
stoletja med Krišno in Kristusom.
Mogoče brezbožni grmi tega ne opazijo.
Kaj pa visoke krošnje? Zviti barok –
čarovnikov nečak.

65.

Form and the age are misting away.
What is a house
if it has no palm cupped for a glittering tear?
When the soul doesn't quicken the body, letters
too will fade in coiled scrolls.
In our blood we are human, and for that reason
all that must happen will enter in.
Flames are flames.
And will sing like fire.

66.

Two baroque hearts show up quietly.
How can I scribe repentance? Or fame?
Or strike with a pencil? How taste living water?
Print both palace and spirit?
How do I know that words will carve out my story
with precision? When I collapse back into habit,
I'm simply copying life.
A tiger's not extraordinary, to share breakfast with one is to erase
the centuries between Krishna and Christ.
Perhaps godless bushes don't see this.
And high treetops? Cunning twists of baroque –
the magician's nephew.

67.

Eliot je pri povzdigovanju.
Auden tudi.
Kdo položi roko na klasično dušo in zapoje:
Zlati pes je bil jelen, ki je pel.
Prižiga sveče,
zahteva cvetje.
Njegov amen plaho namiguje.
Z uglajeno ustrašenostjo?
Ne, s tistim, kar si upa!
Z držo, ki jo je zatajil kakor Savel.
Ti si kralj, ki je osvojil svet.
Mimo tečejo fantički. Hitijo na semenj.
Ne upajo si mimo brezna,
ker ne dihajo skladno s svojo vrsto.

Tomažu za šestdeset let

68.

Užitki so okultni in bistri. Vhodni portali tudi.
So kraji, ki jih ni?
V mestu je še eno mesto in še eno.
V reki še en tok. Še dva.
Zvok se dvigne naenkrat,
spušča pa se počasi,
kakor bela potka v vrtu.

67.

Eliot sees the host held high.
Auden is there too.
To lay hands on a classical soul and sing :
the golden dog was once a stag that sang.
He is lighting candles,
demanding flowers.
His amen is shyly insinuating.
With perfected fear?
No, with what he dares!
With a bearing that he renounced like Saul.
You are the King who conquered the world.
Boys are rushing past, trying to get to the fair.
They don't dare go near the abyss,
because they're not at one with their own breath.

To Tomaž for his sixtieth birthday

68.

Pleasures are occult and lucid. Main portals too.
Are there places that don't yet exist?
In one town, another and then again another.
In one river, still one further stream. Or two.
And noise intensifies all at once,
but then sinks slowly back,
a white path down through the garden.

69.

Od usode sem preč.
V stari skledi se na azelejinih poganjkih nabere
nov saten. Še ena je na skrinji.
Slišim dušo, ki pred vrati presunljivo joka,
ker hoče sem. Zahteva stoletje,
v stolih in vazah košato – z balkoni,
da lahko ribič s palico šviga po nebeški gladini.
Pesnik je naročnik in umetnik. To ni lahko.

18.11.2000
Gregorju Strniši za sedemdeset let

70.

Ko začno prepadi klicati prepad,
se šatuljice same zaklenejo.
Grom premakne rudo in rodove,
da bi tema shranila preteklost.
Človek se boji svinca in odpovedi,
trepeta pred svetlobo.
Naenkrat ga zasujeta dvom in hrepenenje.
Ne more jesti kruha.

69.

I'm smitten by destiny.
In an old vase, on shoots of azalea, fresh satin
forms. Another one, there on the trunk.
I can hear a soul's piercing cry outside the door.
Because it wants in. It would take a century
exuberant with vases and chairs, with balconies,
before a fisherman could cast his rod across the celestial heavens.
A poet is an angler and an artist. It's not easy.

18.11.2000
To Gregor Strniša for his seventieth birthday

70.

When abysses begin to summon the abyss,
small caskets lock themselves shut.
Thunder shifts hearth and heritage
that darkness should preserve the past.
We are afraid of lead and abstinence,
we shudder in the face of light.
We are overcome with doubt and yearning.
We can no longer stomach bread.

71.

Kakor moja mama, kakor vrsta žensk v mestu,
počasi stepam testo, ker hočem, da dobro vzhaja.
Ne maram hiteti,
čeprav me puste ulice zmrazijo do kosti.
Če mi bodo vprašanja usahnila,
ne bom dobila, tistega kar mi pripada.
Čas duše je čas pesmi.
Prostora sta enaka.
Postrežeta si in gresta naprej.

72.

Ob reki se kujata kazen in zveličanje.
Maj poslušam. Odriva stavke.
Naj vprašam kneza o pravici?
Viteza o ropu?
Naj meščan pove o krivi prisegi?
Pesnik o laži in zavisti?
Kaj naj z mladeničem, ki se baha, ker je šibak,
in božjega ne razume?
Okoli vratu nosi *corno da caccia*.

71.

Like my mother, and other women before her,
I knead dough slowly and want it to rise well.
I don't want it to be rushed.
Even if deserted streets chilled me to the bone.
If my questions run dry,
what's really mine won't come to me.
The time of the soul is the time of the poem.
Their spaces overlap. They
take what they need and move on.

72.

By the river, punishment sulks with salvation.
I cock my ear to May. Pushing sentences away.
So, should a prince be asked about justice?
Or a knight about robbery?
Should a burgher talk of false oaths?
Or a poet of lies and jealousy?
And what of the youth who brags because he's so callow
and doesn't understand that god matters?
Around his neck he's wearing a *corno da caccia*.

73.

Če študiram nebesa, vidim, kako misel nastaja.
Sreča mi umije srce.
Zagledam usodo, ki je bolj nežna kakor zrela jagoda.
Nobene poti nazaj ni. Primem jo z dvema prstoma.
Rdeči sok kaplja po kamnu.
Pritisk ne skrivi duha, če hočeš, te požene,
celo tja, kamor še ne bi smel.
Zlatniki v temelju čakajo. Tudi sladkost
na nebu nabrana.
To je zgodovina plodov in sonca, ki sije nanje.

Alešu za štiridest let

74.

Ob zori najdem slepega kenguruja, ki se zaganja v ograjo.
Če ga pustim, bo do večera umrl.
Koliko dela, da bo življenje iz safirja
zraslo v smokvo.
Iz drevesa v mačko. Iz slona v brata.
Med Atenami in Amsterdamom leži
bridkost. Lepotica se boji
starega zlobneža,
ki hoče z odrekanjem razgaliti njen rod.
Esenca pa ves čas kaplja z belih gora.

73.

If I study the heavens, I can see how thoughts emerge.
Happiness lathers my heart.
I see fate more gentle than a ripened strawberry.
There's no turning back. I hold it between two fingers.
Red juices drip onto the stone.
Stress doesn't break the spirit. If you let it, it will push
you, even to where you shouldn't go.
Gold coins suspended in the foundations.
Sweetness, too, gathering in the skies.
This is the history of fruit, with the sun shining down.

To Aleš for his fortieth birthday

74.

At dawn I find a blind kangaroo hurling himself against a fence.
If I let him, he will die by the time it's evening.
Such an effort for life to grow from a sapphire
into a fig tree. From a tree
into a cat. From an elephant into a brother.
Between Athens and Amsterdam lies
affliction. A beauty fears
the saturnine evil one,
who plots to expose her lineage by denial.
But all along essence is dripping from the white mountains.

75.

Po hodnikih odmeva:
Zmagati! Zmagati!
Priboriti si slavo!
Sama opustošena lepota.
Samostan še varujeta Marija in njena srna.
Želod in trava sta polna njunih odtenkov.
Čeprav bojevniki vidijo,
da se zgodovina preklaplja,
si črna mesečina ne upa počastiti ženske,
ki pod kupolo spokojno rojeva.

76.

Jeza in bes
ne obnavljata stvarstva.
Meč poka od občutkov,
ki preskakujejo z električno močjo.
Na ruševine tiho dežuje.
Ker so jih sladke robide varovale,
bo samota s svojim poželenjem obnovila sobane.
Modri sroboti se bodo zazibali v veder dan.
Kaj bršljan vidi, ko iz groba vstane?

    31. 12. 1937, West Glamorgan, Wales

75.

It echoes down the corridor:
To win! To win!
To clamour for fame!
One vast devastated vision.
The monastery still watched over by Mary and her doe.
Acorns and grasses full of their traces.
Even though warriors can
see that history switches course,
this black moonlight does not dare honour the woman
calmly giving birth under the dome.

76.

Anger and fury
aren't going to restore creation.
A sword cracks from emotion
which leaps with an electric charge.
It is raining quietly over the ruins.
Because sweet blackberries shielded them,
solitude will restore the rooms with its desire.
Blue clematis will swing onto the clearness of day.
What does ivy see when it climbs out of the grave?

31.12.1937 West Glamorgan, Wales

Plemenitaš opisuje svoja posestva,
čeprav mu nomadi z rušenjem dokazujejo nov red.
Ne poznajo njegovega razburkanega življenja.
Ne slišijo moči, s katero stopi v samostan.
Nič ne vedo o prehodu med zidom in zrakom?
Preden barbar razume, kako misliti
v pesmi, platnu, glini, kamnu,
uniči vse dame in darove.
Kakšna misel!
Povezati ga z ostanki nebeškega sveta.

77.

A nobleman is describing his estates
even though nomads are wrecking it to define a new order.
They don't know about his stormy life.
They can't sense the verve with which he steps inside a monastery.
Don't they know about the passageways between the walls
        and air?
Before a barbarian knows how to think
in a poem, on canvas, in clay or stone,
he ruins all the ladies and their gifts.
What a thought!
To link him with the remnants of the heavenly world.

BIOGRAPHICAL NOTES

META KUŠAR, poet and essayist, was born in Ljubljana in 1952. With four collections of poetry in print and with many poems in anthologies and literary magazines, she is one of Slovenia's most popular and successful women poets. Her latest collection *Jaspis* (Jasper) was published by Apokalipsa in 2008 and a selection has since been translated into German. *Ljubljana* was tranlated into Slovak in 2008. Her most recent publication is a book of interviews with a range of prominent Slovene artists she has interviewed over the last decade.Since 1980 she has regularly contributed to the Slovene National Radio and the RAI-Trieste with cultural and historical talks. Occasionally she writes film scripts and directs them and she has also directed a musical performance of her poetry, 'The Throne of Poetry', which was staged in Slovenia, Washington (1991) and London (2000).

ANA JELNIKAR was born in Slovenia in 1975 and shared her education between London and Ljubljana. She has recently completed her PhD from the School of Oriental and African Studies, University of London researching the links between the Indian poet Rabindranath Tagore and the Slovenian poet Srečko Kosovel. She translates into both Slovene and English and co-translated Arc's anthology *Six Slovenian Poets*, and her co-translation with Barbara Siegel Carlson of Srečko Kosovel's *Look Back Look Ahead* was published by Ugly Duckling Presse (New York) in 2010.

STEPHEN WATTS is a poet, editor & translator, with family roots in the Italian Alps. He lives in Whitechapel. He twice won second prize in the National Poetry Competition (1983 and 1992). Recent books of his own work include *Gramsci & Caruso* (2004), *The Blue Bag* (2005), *Mountain Language / Lingua di montagna* (2009), *The Language Of It* (DVD

113

2007), and a video-poem *Journey To My Father* (2009). He edited Amarjit Chandan's *Sonata For Four Hands* (2010) and has co-translated poetry by A. N. Stencl (2007), Ziba Karbassi (2009), Adnan al-Sayegh (2009) and Meta Kušar (2010). He has worked extensively as a poet in schools and hospitals in East London and in 2006 worked with HI-Arts in Inverness on social issues of suicide and survival. In 2007 he was awarded an Arts Council grant for his writing and research and at present is completing a new edition of *Mother Tongues* (Bloodaxe Books, due 2012) which anthologises some of the many fine poets in the UK who write in languages other than English. He is also completing an extensive on-line bibliography of modern poetry in English translation.

FRANCIS R. JONES studied Serbo-Croat and German at Cambridge University, modern Yugoslav poetry at Sarajevo University (1977-78), and language learning / teaching methodology at Reading and Newcastle University. He is now a senior lecturer at Newcastle University, where he teaches translation studies, and researches the role of the poetry translator as creative rewriter and socio-political actor. He has published fifteen solo-translated volumes of poetry translations, mainly from Bosnian-Croatian-Serbian into English, but also from Dutch, Hungarian and Russian. He has also translated from French, German, Papiamento and Sranan, and into Northumbrian and Yorkshire dialect. He has been winner or runner-up for nine solo or team translation prizes in the UK, the USA, the Netherlands and Bosnia.

Also available in the Arc Publications
'VISIBLE POETS' series (Series Editor: Jean Boase-Beier)

No. 1 – MIKLÓS RADNÓTI (Hungary)
Camp Notebook
Translated by Francis R. Jones, introduced by George Szirtes

No. 2 – BARTOLO CATTAFI (Italy)
Anthracite
Translated by Brian Cole, introduced by Peter Dale
(Poetry Book Society Recommended Translation)

No. 3 – MICHAEL STRUNGE (Denmark)
A Virgin from a Chilly Decade
Translated by Bente Elsworth, introduced by John Fletcher

No. 4 – TADEUSZ RÓŻEWICZ (Poland)
recycling
Translated by Barbara Bogoczek (Plebanek) & Tony Howard,
introduced by Adam Czerniawski

No. 5 – CLAUDE DE BURINE (France)
Words Have Frozen Over
Translated by Martin Sorrell, introduced by Susan Wicks

No. 6 – CEVAT ÇAPAN (Turkey)
Where Are You, Susie Petschek?
Translated by Cevat Çapan & Michael Hulse,
introduced by A. S. Byatt

No. 7 – JEAN CASSOU (France)
33 Sonnets of the Resistance
With an original introduction by Louis Aragon
Translated by Timothy Adès, introduced by Alistair Elliot

No. 8 – ARJEN DUINKER (Holland)
The Sublime Song of a Maybe
Translated by Willem Groenewegen, introduced by Jeffrey Wainwright

No. 9 – MILA HAUGOVÁ (Slovakia)
Scent of the Unseen
Translated by James & Viera Sutherland-Smith,
introduced by Fiona Sampson

No. 10 – ERNST MEISTER (Germany)
Between Nothing and Nothing
Translated by Jean Boase-Beier, introduced by John Hartley Williams

No. 21 – ELI TOLARETXIPI (Spain / Basque)
Still Life with Loops
Translated by Philip Jenkins, introduced by Robert Crawford

No. 22 – FERNANDO KOFMAN (Argentina)
The Flights of Zarza
Translated by Ian Taylor, introduced by Andrew Graham Yooll

No. 23 – LARISSA MILLER (Russia)
Guests of Eternity
Translated by Richard McKane, introduced by Sasha Dugdale
(Poetry Book Society Recommended Translation)

No. 24 – ANISE KOLTZ (Luxembourg)
At the Edge of Night
Translated by Anne-Marie Glasheen, introduced by Caroline Price

No. 25 – MAURICE CARÊME (Belgium)
Defying Fate
Translated by Christopher Pilling, introduced by Martin Sorrell

No. 26 – VALÉRIE ROUZEAU (France)
Cold Spring in Winter
Translated by Susan Wicks, introduced by Stephen Romer
(2010 Griffin Poetry Prize Short-list)
(2010 Oxford-Weidenfeld Translation Prize Short-list)

No. 27 – RAZMIK DAVOYAN (France)
Whispers and Breath of the Meadows
Translated by Arminé Tamrazian, introduced by W. N. Herbert

No. 28 – FRANÇOIS JACQMIN (Belgium)
The Book of the Snow
Translated by Philip Mosely, introduced by Clive Scott

No. 29 – KRISTIINA EHIN (Estonia)
The Scent of Your Shadow
Translated by Ilmar Lehtpere, introduced by Sujata Bhatt
(Poetry Book Society Recommended Translation)